Be a
History
Detective

Tudor Home

Dereen Taylor

WAYLAND

This book is a differentiated text version of
The History Detective Investigates Tudor Home
by Alan Childs

This edition first published in 2009 by Wayland

Wayland
Hachette Children's Books
338 Euston Road
London NW1 3BH

Wayland Australia
Level 17/207 Kent Street
Sydney NSW 2000

Editor: Victoria Brooker
Designer: Simon Borrough

British Library Cataloguing in Publication Data:
  Taylor, Dereen
  Tudor home. - Differentiated ed. - (Be a history
detective)
  1. Dwellings - England - History -
16th century - Juvenile literature
  2. Housing - England - History -16th century -
Juvenile literature
  3. England - Social conditions - 16th century -
Juvenile literature
  4. England - Social life and customs - 16th century -
Juvenile literature
  I. Title II. Childs, Alan, 1942-
392.3 '6 'o42 '09031

ISBN: 978 0 7502 5704 6

Printed and bound in China

Wayland is a division of Hachette Children's Books,
an Hachette UK Company.

www.hachettelivre.co.uk

Picture acknowledgements:
The publishers would like to thank the
following for permission to reproduce their
pictures: Alan Childs 7 (right), 10 (right);
GGS Photographics 19 (left); Hulton Getty
Picture Library 19; Ingatestone Hall cover,
26, 27 (top & bottom); The Bridgeman Art
Library 4, 5 (top) (Mark Fiennes), 13 (right),
14, 16 (bottom) (Christie's Images), 17, 18,
23; The Fotomas Index Picture Library 25;
Mary Evans Picture Library 20 (bottom), 24,
29; Museum of London 13 (left), 16 (top), 19
(bottom); National Trust Photographic
Library: 1, 28 (Andrew Butler), 22 (bottom)
(Andrea Jones), 21 (Nadia MacKenzie), 4
(bottom) (John Miller), cover 6, 11 (left)
(Geoff Morgan), cover, 9 (top & bottom) (Erik
Pelham), 22 (top) (Mike Williams), cover
(Rupert Truman); Royal Collection 15
(bottom); Weald and Downland Museum 7
(left), 8, 12; Wayland Picture Library, 10
(right), 15 (top), 20 (top).

Contents

Tudor homes   4

Building Tudor homes   6

Tudor chimneys   8

Tudor windows   10

Tudor beds   12

Tudor toilets   14

Washing   16

Tudor kitchens   18

Inside Tudor homes   20

Tudor gardens   22

Town houses   24

Ingatestone Hall   26

Your project   28

Glossary   30

Answers   30

Books to read   31

Places to visit   31

Index   32

Tudor homes

Imagine a home where the toilet was a plank over a pit and where glass windows were so valuable they were left in a will! That's what some Tudor homes were like.

Building materials

The Tudor period lasted from 1485 to 1603. In 1485, timber was used to build houses. However, by the time Elizabeth I became queen in 1558, many trees had been cut down and not replanted. This made timber very expensive. Luckily, bricks became cheap enough for many people to use instead.

The history detective, Sherlock Bones, will help you to find clues and collect evidence about Tudor homes. Wherever you see one of Sherlock's paw-prints, there is a mystery to solve. The answers can be found on pages 30 and 31.

▼ *This painting from about 1570 shows different types of Tudor houses.*

Different-sized houses

The smallest Tudor houses have not survived. These were tiny cottages built of wood and clay. Only the bigger houses still stand today. Burghley House in Lincolnshire is one of the finest. William Cecil built it between 1565 and 1587.

Detective work

Try to find Tudor houses in your area. Your local library may be able to help. They may not look like Tudor buildings now, but there are clues for the careful history detective!

▲ Burghley House is built from limestone.

▲ A Tudor cottage.

❖ Why do you think the smallest Tudor houses have not survived?

An Italian visitor described how the English built their homes:

First they construct a frame of wood joined together with wooden pegs and then between one layer of wood and another they put bricks. The houses have many windows in which they put glass that's almost as clear as crystal. Inside, the houses are... decorated with wood carving... On the floors they put straw...

Alessandro Magno, 1562

Building Tudor homes

Timbered Tudor houses were made of different levels. Each level jutted out a bit further than the one below. The overhangs were called **jetties**. Sometimes, townhouses were so close together at the top, you could shake hands with your neighbour across the street!

Detective work

Find examples of timbered houses or farm buildings in books and on the Internet. Make drawings or take photos of the beam patterns. Can you find examples of jetties?

◀ *Building started on Little Moreton Hall (left) in the 1440s. It was finally completed in 1580.*

✿ Why do you think Tudor houses were built with jetties?

Wooden beams

Little Moreton Hall has fantastic patterns made from wooden beams. In Tudor times, the beams were often left as natural wood.

One Tudor man came home to find that a rich neighbour had moved his house. His son tells the story:

'My father had a garden... and a house... this house they loosed from the ground, and bare (carried) upon rollers into my father's garden 22 feet (over six metres) ... No warning was given to him.'

John Stowe, *A Survey of London*, 1598

Timbered houses

The Tudors used newly cut oak, elm or ash wood to build a timbered house. Tree trunks were laid across a **saw-pit** and cut with a huge two-man saw. Carpenters often cut all the joints for a new house in their yard. They numbered them so that they could be put together on the building site.

▲ Can you see the carpenter's marks on the beams above? These made sure that each piece of wood was put in the right place.

◀ In later houses, bricks were used to fill the gaps between beams.

Wattle and daub

In early Tudor houses, the spaces between the wooden frame were filled with small woven sticks called 'wattle'. These were covered with a 'daub' of mud, clay and cow-dung, mixed with straw or cow hair. Making the walls was a messy, smelly job!

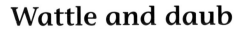

Tudor chimneys

Detective work

If you can visit a large Tudor house, look at the chimneys carefully, perhaps using binoculars. See how the bricks make up a design and sketch some of the designs you find.

Chimneys had been around for centuries, but they were still very rare in Tudor times. Most early houses had one big room, with a smoke hole in the roof. Fires were made in the middle of the room. Smoke then had to find its way out of the smoke hole, or through cracks and windows. This meant most homes were full of smoke and soot.

▼ *This early flint and thatched cottage has the type of smoke hole that was used during Tudor times.*

One Tudor writer said that old men living in his village noted great changes in the houses:

'One [change] is the multitude of chimneys lately erected, ...in their young days there were not above two or three...'

William Harrison, *A Description of England*, 1577—87

✿ Why do you think it was easier to build the first chimneys on to the ends of houses?

◀ *This Tudor house has an end chimney.*

▼ *Fireplaces made it easier to burn coal. This gave more heat than wood, so homes were warmer.*

Brick chimneys

Cheap bricks made it possible for the Tudors to become the first people to use chimneys in most houses. At first, it was easier to add chimneys on to an end wall. Later, chimneys were built at the same time as the house.

Room upstairs

Chimneys changed people's lives. There were no more smoky rooms and homes could have rooms upstairs. The extra floor could be built because smoke no longer had to find its way out of the smoke hole.

Tudor windows

Glass was too expensive for many Tudors. The word window means 'wind eye' – an eye for the wind to blow through. In the days before glass, this is just what the wind did!

Window covers

By Tudor times, glass was becoming more common in rich homes. But other window covers, like wooden shutters and oiled cloth, were still used. Sometimes, windows were covered with reeds or pieces of thin stone. When these windows were closed, the rooms were dark and when they were open, the rooms were often cold!

▲ **Lattice windows** *could be very plain…*

◀ *… or very ornamental.*

❧ Do you think that the designs in the windows on the left mean something?

Valuable windows

Glass windows were very valuable and had to be protected. Some owners of grand houses removed and stored their windows when they were not at home.

Detective work

Visit an old church and look at the windows. See how small pieces of glass are held in place by metal strips. This is how Tudor windows were made. Compare these windows to modern lattice windows. How are they different?

The house-builder Elizabeth of Shrewsbury had so many windows in her Tudor mansion that it was said: 'Hardwick Hall, more glass than wall'.

▼ *Hardwick Hall was built between 1591 and 1597.*

'Of old time, our country houses, instead of glass did use much lattice... But... our lattices are also grown into less use, because glass is come to be so plentiful.'

William Harrison,
A Description of England,
1577-87

❖ The owner of Hardwick Hall put her initials all over the house. Can you spot any of them?

Tudor beds

Tudor houses often had no landings. One upstairs room led into another. The large expensive beds were called '**testers**' or four-posters. They had curtains around them to keep out draughts and protect people's privacy!

▶ *'Tester' beds were high off the ground. There was room underneath to store a* **'truckle'** *bed. It was pulled out at night for a servant or child to sleep on.*

Detective work

Contact your County Record Office and ask if they have any Tudor **inventories** for your area. They may have a translation or you may have to read real Tudor handwriting! The bedstead is usually listed with the bed linen and hangings.

Beds in wealthy homes

To a Tudor, the word 'bed' probably just meant the mattress. The wooden frame was called a 'bedstead'. The mattress might be stuffed with wool, feathers or straw.

A strange, but cheap filling for pillows and mattresses was thistledown – the furry seeds of the thistle:

'The common thistle, wherof the greatest quantity of down is gathered for divers (various) purposes, as well by the poor to stop (stuff) pillows, cushions, and beds for want of feathers, as also bought of the rich upholsters to mix with the feathers and down they do sell...'

John Gerard, *Historie of Plants*, 1597

Why was thistledown mixed with feathers to make a stuffing for pillows? There are clues in the text above.

▶ *The bed of a very rich Tudor.*

◀ *A Tudor warming pan.*

Heating beds

When the nights were cold, Tudors heated their beds with hot coals in a warming pan.

Beds in poor homes

Beds for poor people were simple wooden frames with ropes criss-crossed to support the mattress.

As beds were valuable, the Tudors often left them in their wills.

Tudor toilets

▲ *Indoor toilets were built out from the side of the house, with a pit below.*

Tudors went to the toilet where it suited them — by the roadside, in the river or even in their own fireplace! It was called 'plucking a rose'. They emptied their chamber pots out of windows into the street below.

Toilet names

The Tudor word for a toilet was 'jakes'. It was also known as a 'privy' and a 'stool room'. A toilet was often a plank over a pit in the garden. An indoor toilet was just a tiny room with a plank over a pit lined with ashes.

Emptying toilets

When the toilet was full, it had to be emptied. The 'jakes farmer' cleared it out. They mixed the contents with the ashes. This was then used as fertilizer.

'Hookers' were Tudor thieves who used long hooks to steal people's clothes. One hooker hooked a chamber pot by mistake!

'...his face, his head, and his neck were all besmeared... so he stunk worse than a jakes-farmer...'

Robert Greene, *The Black Book's Messenger*, 1592

▲ *Hampton Court Palace (above) had a 14-seater toilet!*

Flushing toilets

In 1596, Sir John Harrington invented the first flushing toilet. Queen Elizabeth ordered one for Richmond Palace.

▶ *This strange object is called a '**close stool**'.*

🐾 What do you think this 'close stool' was used for?

Detective work

Find out more about the history of toilets. The books listed on page 31 will help.

Washing

Washing was not something that Tudors did every day. Only someone as important as a king or queen had a proper bathroom. Rich Tudors bathed in a wooden tub in front of their bedroom fire. Poor people took a quick bath in a pond or river!

▲ A small sweet-smelling pomander.

Pomanders

Some people carried **'pomanders'** round with them. These were full of sweet herbs to hide everyone else's body smells.

Soap

Rich people with baths could afford soap scented with almond or musk oil. Most people made their own soap for washing their clothes and themselves. This was a smelly job. Water that had been trickled through burnt wood ash was strained and mixed with animal fat.

▲ Rich Tudors, like the painter Isaac Oliver, wore grand clothes, but bathed very little.

Washing clothes

Many Tudors washed their clothes in a wash-house by a river. Clothes were beaten clean with 'battling stones'.

Tooth soap

Many Tudors had smelly breath because of their bad teeth. Even Queen Elizabeth's teeth were black and rotten. Tudors used a tooth soap to clean their teeth. It was made from honey, vinegar and white wine and probably did not help their teeth much!

▼ *Having teeth pulled out was very painful in Tudor times.*

Detective work

Can you guess why none of Elizabeth I's portraits show her bad teeth?

This is a recipe for Tudor soap:

'*The leaves of the bramble boiled in water, with honey, alum (salt) and a little white wine... make a most excellent lotion... and the decoction fastneth [the boiled mixture strengthens] the teeth.*'

John Gerald, *Herbal*, 1597

Tudor kitchen

Detective work
Find a book of Tudor
recipes (see page 31).
Do you know any of
the ingredients?

Early Tudor houses had just one big room where
everyone lived and slept. Food was cooked here over
an open fire. When houses were divided into **storeys**
there was space for a kitchen.

▲ *This painting shows many
types of Tudor food.*

The kitchen fire

Everything was cooked on the kitchen fire. At night the fire
was covered with a lid, then it was poked back into life the
next morning. In large kitchens there were **spits** for turning
meat. Sometimes a dog was put in a tread-wheel and had to
keep walking to turn the meat until it was cooked.

Tudor food

Rich Tudors ate every kind of meat, from roast swan to wild boar. They also ate white bread. Poor people ate brown bread. Cheap vegetables made up most of their diet. All Tudors tried not to eat fresh fruit – they thought it would upset their stomachs. Most Tudors loved puddings. They ate gingerbread decorated with real gold and marzipan. Beer was very popular. Servants were allowed a gallon (4.5 litres) a day. Ladies drank the less bitter ale – and so did children!

◄ This food cupboard has air holes to help keep food fresh.

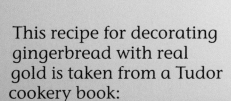

This recipe for decorating gingerbread with real gold is taken from a Tudor cookery book:

'Take and cut your leaf of gold... into square pieces like dice, and with a... cony's (rabbit's) tail's end moisted (wet) a little, take the gold up by one corner, lay it on the place being first made moist...'

▲ This wooden mould leaves the shape of a drummer on top of a cake.

Inside Tudor homes

Most people did not have much furniture. They just had a bed, a table, a chair, some stools and a chest for storing things. Most Tudor furniture was solid and plain and made of oak. Floors were made of tile or stone. In the country, they were often just bare earth covered with straw.

▲ *In poor homes benches and stools were used more than chairs like this one.*

Detective work

Look at any Tudor paintings showing the inside of houses. Make a list of the furniture and objects and try to work out what they were used for.

❀ What game are the children playing in the picture below?

▼ *Children playing games in the long gallery of a Tudor home.*

Lighting up

Chimneys and windows made Tudor homes warmer and brighter. After dark, candles or **rushlights** were used for light. Most people made their own candles from animal fat.

The gallery

In small houses, the 'hall' was used for sitting or playing games. Large houses had a long gallery where families listened to music being performed. Children could also play games that needed lots of space.

▲ *Carpets were too expensive to walk over. This carpet has been laid on a table for decoration.*

Wall decorations

Wallpaper was made after about 1520, but it was very expensive. Rooms were made more colourful by travelling painters. Rich families could afford to panel walls, plaster ceilings and hang tapestries. Even the poor had painted cloths on their walls.

Compare this description of floors in English houses with Alessandro Magno's on page 5. Had things improved by Magno's time?

The floors are strewed with clay... covered with rushes which are now and then renewed... the foundation... sometimes remains for twenty years nursing a collection of spittle, vomits, excrement of dogs and human beings... and other filth.

Erasmus, 1518

Tudor gardens

▲ *A Tudor knot garden.*

During Tudor times, explorers came back from trips all around the world with new plants. 'Love-apples' (tomatoes), potatoes and apricots arrived in Britain. Flowers like laburnum and Christmas roses arrived too. Tudor gardens were already filled with hollyhocks, irises and marigolds. Flowers were not just for decoration. Their petals were also used in cookery and medicine.

Garden design

Owners of large gardens loved to create gardens with magical patterns. There were knot gardens, which looked like tapestry designs and mazes where hidden fountains might squirt you. Rich Tudors liked to decorate their gardens with stone statues and hedges that were snipped and shaped into fantastic designs.

▼ *It must have been difficult for gardeners to keep this Tudor garden in shape.*

A royal garden

At Hampton Court, Henry VIII put small green-and-white fences round the flowerbeds. He also placed stone animals everywhere. In the gardens of other Tudor mansions, like Ingatestone Hall, there were pavilions or summer houses.

Vegetable gardens

Poor people had gardens and fields round their cottages where they grew flax for making linen. Both large and small houses also grew food to eat. Carrots and turnips were used to make thick soups and herbs were used for flavouring and medicine. Caraway seeds were eaten with 'pippin' apples, which we still have today.

In William Shakespeare's play, *King Henry IV – Part II* (Act V Scene III), Justice Shallow shows friends around his orchard:

'Nay, you shall see mine orchard, where... we will eat a last year's pippin (apple) of my own graffing (growing), with a dish of caraways (caraway seeds)...'

◀ *Apricots were a new type of fruit in Tudor times.*

Town houses

London grew quickly during Tudor times, but most Tudor towns would still seem very small to us. In 1603, London had a population of 200,000. Today, it has a population of over 7 million.

▲ *A Tudor picture map of 1563. It shows the area around St Paul's Cathedral (top).*

❧ How is the Tudor St Paul's different from the cathedral we know today?

Dirt and disease

Tall houses and jetties made town streets dark and dirty. People were meant to put out a lantern at night and clean up their own rubbish. But many didn't and rats were everywhere. Tudor doctors didn't know that rats caused a terrible disease called the **plague**.

Detective work
Compare the map of London (left) with a modern map. Do any place names appear on both maps?

Rat catchers were kept busy. They shouted these words to get customers:

Rats or mice, ha'ye any rats, mice, polecats or weasles
Or ha'ye any old sows sick of the measles?
I can kill them, and I can kill moles, and I can kill vermin that
Creepeth up and creepeth down, and peepeth into holes.

British Museum

▲ This spectacle maker's shop is in the front room of his house.

Working from home

A town house was often used for trade. The shutters on ground-floor windows could be lowered down to make a shop counter.

Fire!

Risk of fire meant that it was safer to build the kitchen in brick. People were supposed to tile not thatch their roofs to make it more difficult for flames to spread. Everyone had to keep a fire bucket, and a hook to pull down burning thatch.

Ingatestone Hall

Ingatestone Hall is a Tudor house in Essex, England. It was the home of Sir William Petre. He served four Tudor monarchs – without losing his head! His grand house was begun in 1540. The Petre family still live there.

Servants

Life at Ingatestone was like living in a large village. Most jobs were done by someone on the estate. These jobs included rabbit keeping and gardening. The older servants earned £2 a year. They were also given uniforms and their food and lodging.

◀ Sir William Petre.

You had to be rich like Sir William to invite Queen Elizabeth I to stay because she brought hundreds of people with her. This is a small part of the list of supplies needed to look after the queen for four days. The full list was 20 times as long:

1 dozen wax lights, weight 3lb (1.4kg)
6 cygnets
27 geese
French wine, 10 gallons (45.5 litres)
7 gallons (32 litres) of cream
44 dishes of butter
693 eggs
200 oranges

Ingatestone Hall

Special rooms

Like many Tudor houses, Ingatestone was built around a courtyard. There were special rooms for everything: a salt-house for keeping salt dry and a still-room for preparing herbs. The dairy and the bakery were the most important work rooms. In one week 76kg of cheese might be eaten. In one year, the bakers might bake 20,000 loaves of bread!

▲ *Games were played in the long gallery at Ingatestone.*

❉ Why was salt so important in Tudor times?

▼ *There was always fresh fish from the pond to serve at the table at Ingatestone Hall.*

Your project

You should have found plenty of clues in the detective work at the end of each section. These clues will help you to do your own project about a Tudor home.

First, you will need to choose a topic. You could use one of the questions below to help you start.

Topic questions
1. How were different Tudor homes built?
2. Compared to houses today, what rooms might be missing in an ordinary Tudor house?
3. What furniture would you expect to find in a Tudor house?

▼ *Half-timbered Tudor cottages.*

When you have got together all your information, present it in an interesting way. You could use one of the ideas below.

Project presentation

• Make a model of a timbered house. Use two different-sized shoe boxes, stuck bottom to bottom, to make the 'jetty'.

• Pretend you live in Tudor times. Write a letter to a cousin, telling them all about your house.

• Write a play and invent a scene where Elizabeth I attends a banquet at a grand house.

▼ *A lively Tudor party in a banqueting hall.*

Glossary

close stool a small toilet, like a box.

inventories lists of people's possessions when they died.

jetties where the storeys on buildings jut out further than the ones beneath.

lattice windows windows with diamond-shaped panes.

plague a killer infection carried by rat fleas.

pomanders holders for sweet-smelling herbs.

rushlight a wall light made from a rush dipped in tallow.

saw-pit a pit where trees can be sawed.

spit a thin pointed bar on which meat is cooked over an open fire.

storeys a floor or level in a building.

testers beds with a roof; a four-poster bed.

truckle a movable bed.

Answers

Page 5: The smallest homes were just made of clay, wattle and daub and straw-thatch with no proper floors. They fell down and rotted over the years.

Page 6: This could have been to make more room or to shelter the lower floors from bad weather.

Page 9: It was easier because a wall was already there to support the new chimney brickwork. Moving the fire to one end also made more space inside the house.

Page 10: The windows are very decorative. Rich families used their 'coat of arms' in the design, as in this picture. This showed how important they were.

Page 11: If you look carefully, she has put her initials (E.S.) into the stonework on the top of the house.

Page 13: Upholsterers were cheating people by pretending their pillows were full of expensive feathers. Instead they had added thistledown, which was free.

Page 15: It is a toilet, specially padded for a royal bottom!

Page 20: They are playing nine pins. This is how our games of skittles and ten-pin bowling started.

Page 24: Our St Paul's was rebuilt after the one shown here burnt down in the Great Fire of London in 1666. The new St Paul's has a round dome instead of a square tower.

Page 27: There were no fridges in Tudor times to keep food fresh. Salt was used for preserving food.

Books to read

Creative History Activity Packs: Tudors
by Jane Bower (David Fulton 2002)

Superloo: Henry VIII's Privy
by W. C. Flushing (Puffin 2007)

The Tudors in Britain
by Robert Hull (Wayland 2007)

History from Buildings: Tudor Britain
by Stewart Ross (Watts 2006)

Reconstructed: The Tudors
by Liz Gogerly (Wayland 2005)

Tudor Life: Homes
by Nicola Barber (Wayland, 2009)

Tudor Cookery: Recipes and History by Peter Brears (English Heritage 2004)

Places to visit

Cowdray House
River Ground Stables,
Cowdray Park, Midhurst,
West Sussex GU29 9AL
www.cowdray.org.uk
Cowdray is an early Tudor courtier's palace where you can explore the Tudor kitchens, splendid gatehouse and visitor centre.
Royal visitors there included Henry VIII and Elizabeth I.

Little Moreton Hall
Congleton,
Cheshire CW12 4SD
One of Britain's finest timber-framed moated manor houses.

Hardwick Hall
Doe Lea,
Chesterfield,
Derbyshire S44 5QJ
Hardwick Hall contains a large collection of Tudor furniture, paintings and tapestries.

Index

Numbers in **bold** refer to pictures and captions

banquet 29, **29**
bathroom 16
beams 6, **6,** 7
beds 12–13, **12,** 13, **13,** 20
    four-poster (see tester)
    tester 12, **12**
bricks 4, **4,** 5, 7, 8, 9, 25
building 4, 6–7 , 9, 25, 28
Burghley House 5, **5**

candles 20
carpet 21, **21**
chamber pot 14
chimneys 8–9, **9,** 20
church **4,** 11, 24, **24**
close-stool (see toilet)
clothes 14, 16, 17
cottages **4,** 5, **5,** 8, **8, 28**
courtyard 27
curtains 12

Elizabeth I, Queen of England 4, 17, 26, 29

fireplace 9, **9,** 14, 16, 18
floor 5, 20, 21
food 18, **18,** 19, 22, 23, **23,** 26, 27
furniture 12, **12,** 13, **13,** 19, 20, 28

gallery 20, **20,** 27
garden 14, 22–23, **22,** 27
glass 10, 11

Hampton Court Palace 15, **15,** 23
Hardwick Hall 11, **11**
Henry VIII, King of England 23

Ingatestone Hall 23, 26–27, **27**

jetties 6, **6,** 24, 29

kitchen 18–19, **18,** 25

Little Moreton Hall 6, **6**

plague 24
pomander 16, **16**
poor 13, 16, 19, 20

rich 12, 13, **13,** 16, **16,** 19, 21, 26
Richmond Palace 15

servants 12, 26
shops 25, **25**
smoke hole 8, **8,** 9
soap 16, 17

teeth 17, **17**
thatch 4, 25
timber 4, **4,** 5, 6, 7, 28
toilet 4, 14–15, **14, 15**
town 6, 24–25

wallpaper 21
warming pan 13, **13**
wattle and daub 7, **7**
windows 4, 5, 8, 10–11, **10, 11,** 20